The Mission of

the Seventy-Two

Leave No Soul Behind

Personally Reaching Out to

Inactive Catholics

The Mission of the Seventy-Two

Leave No Soul Behind

updated June 2023
Personally Reaching Out to Inactive Catholics

ISBN: 978-1-945423-29-1

Deacon Carl Calcara

Cover Artist: Brenda Calcara Merriman (brendakmerriman@gmail.com)

The Mission of the Seventy-Two

missionofthe72@gmail.com

Printed in the United States

Contents

Foreword...5

Introduction...9

Chapter 1 It Takes One to Know One 15

    The Journey Home.. 18

    A Vocation to the Diaconate................................ 21

Chapter 2 God's Request: 27

Chapter 3 Empowering Active Catholics................. 37

Chapter 4 The Importance of the Sacraments in the Life of a Disciple ... 41

    The Sacrament of Baptism 41

    The Sacrament of Confirmation........................ 46

    The Liturgy of the Mass....................................... 48

    The Sacrament of the Eucharist........................ 52

    The Sacrament of Reconciliation...................... 55

Chapter 5 Praying for Inactive Catholics................. 59

Chapter 6 God Is with Us..65

Conclusion We Are All Called to Be Shepherds of the Good Shepherd 71

Acknowledgement 79

If you have questions or want more information about The Mission of the Seventy-Two go to SaintJohnSunbury.org or send an email to missionofthe72@gmail.com.

Foreword

In Luke's Gospel, Chapter 15, Jesus is criticized by the Pharisees and scribes for spending time with sinners. In response, He tells them a parable about a lost sheep and asks who among them would not leave the ninety-nine in the wilderness and go in search of the one that was lost. Truth be told, not one of them would have gone after the one lost sheep, but would have written it off as the cost of doing business. But, truth be told, Jesus does go after the one lost sheep and carries it back home. Jesus was trying to teach us a different way of living in relationship with God and with one another in a human community.

At one time or another, we have all lost something of value, and finding it again involved actively going out and searching for what was lost. Yet we do so without counting the cost because that which we lost was of great value to us. In like manner, Christ the Good Shepherd goes after each sheep that is lost. All of us are sinners, and we have all, at times, lost our way and wandered away from God. However, even though we were lost, God still valued us and still actively sought us out. We should all thank God for never giving up on us and seeing value in us, even when it seemed like everyone else was busy minding their own business.

The word Christian literally means "follower of Christ," and, as Christians, we are called to act like Christ in the world.

What Christ does for us, we are meant to do for others. Just as Christ sees value in us when we are lost and goes out to seek and find what is lost—us—we are called to do the same. We are called by Christ to see value in those who have become lost to God, who have strayed for whatever reasons from the practice of the Faith, away from the Church and the community of believers.

This is why The Mission of the Seventy-Two is so important. I have personally known Deacon Carl Calcara for fifteen years. God has placed upon his heart a desire to seek and find the lost sheep, the people who are near and dear to us, who once sat in our pews and were active in our parishes. This mission of bringing souls back to Christ and back to the Church that Christ established as His Sheepfold is not reserved for deacons, priests, religious, and bishops. It is a mission that Christ gives to each one of us. He calls us to search for those who are lost, starting with those closest to us, and then going out to all those whom Christ will put in our paths as we walk with Him in our journey to Heaven.

I want to recommend that you consider taking as your way The Mission of the Seventy-Two, both for you as an individual Catholic Christian and for your parish community. The Mission of the Seventy-Two is simple in its work yet profound in its effect. Following the way outlined by The Mission of the Seventy-Two holds incredible potential and power to draw many souls back to the Lord, to literally save and transform lives by each of us reaching out, searching and finding people who have lost their way, offering them our hospitality and care, expressing our love and concern to them, and accompanying them back home. The Mission of the Seventy-Two is not just the mission of the Church or a parish, but a mission that each of us is personally called to accept. And, along the way, we will find ourselves and others very much changed because we saw value in those who had been lost and reached out to them, just as Christ did for us.

Fr. David W. Sizemore

Pastor, St. Francis de Sales Catholic Church, Newark, Ohio

November 2, 2020 – Feast of All Souls

Introduction

As a deacon in the Catholic Church, God has called me to serve as a minister of the Word, a minister of the altar, and a minister of justice and charity. In particular, He has called me to proclaim His Gospel to the world in His mission for the salvation of souls. However, it is only through His incredible grace, mercy, and charity that I gradually came to understand this calling in my life.

Like many Catholics today, there was a time in my life when I took my faith for granted. I let the voices of the world drown out the voice of God in my life. I stopped going to Mass and convinced myself that this was acceptable. However, true to His word, the Lord never left me and gently called me back to the Church and into a relationship with Him.

I have come to realize that God has a plan for each and every one of us. In the Old Testament, speaking to the Israelites in captivity, God said: *"For I know well the plans I have in mind for you . . . plans for your welfare and not for woe, so as to give you a future of hope. When you call me, and come and pray to me, I will listen to you. When you look for me, you will find me. Yes, when you seek me with all your heart, I will let you find me . . . and I will change your lot"* (Jer 29:11–14). The Lord speaks these words to each of us as well.

Yet God has given us free will, and, because of this, He does not control our minds or hearts as His plan unfolds throughout our lives. Rather, He defines our steps within His plan. We read in Proverbs: *"The human heart plans the way, but the Lord directs the steps"* (Prv 16:9). We must have faith that God will direct the plans He has for us because He knows and sees all—God is past, present, and future. There is no time as we know time because with God a thousand years is like a single day. We must remember over the span of our lifetimes that God's plan for each of us happens in His time, not our time.

Over many years of practicing my Catholic Faith, I have thought about my family, friends, neighbors, and fellow parishioners who have stopped practicing the Faith, or choose to attend Mass only on Christmas or Easter. My hope and prayer is and has always been that they will come back to the Church.

After ten years of serving in the diaconate, at the age of fifty-seven, the Lord asked me to personally reach out to inactive Catholics to bring them back to the Church and back to the Most Sacred Liturgy of the Mass. This book is meant to share how God has developed His plan within me over my lifetime.

However, this plan is not only my plan but a mission to which God calls each of us as Christ's disciples. Every Christian is involved in the saving mission of Jesus: to do the will of His Father in Heaven and, by His Incarnation, Life, Passion, Death, and Resurrection, to save all souls for all eternity in

Heaven. And any plan that God has for us involves the mission of the Universal Church, which is the salvation of souls (salus animarum). We are not only responsible for bringing our own souls to Heaven but those of our husbands and wives, our children, grandchildren, brothers and sisters, friends, neighbors, fellow parishioners, and, yes, even strangers.

However, in order for God's plan to work to bring others to salvation in our lives, it is essential that we receive the sacraments that unite us to Christ, and it is essential that we are open to the Holy Spirit working in our lives. Reception of the sacraments—especially participation in the Mass and the frequent reception of Holy Communion—is at the heart of God's plan for us, for we cannot hear what the Lord is asking of us, or live to our full potential in Christ, if we keep our Faith at arm's length and ignore the sacraments. The sacraments and the gifts of the Holy Spirit are woven into God's plan for us and give us what we need to assist us on our journey toward salvation. As we read in the Catechism of the Catholic Church:

The Church affirms that for believers the sacraments of the New Covenant are necessary for salvation (cf. Council of Trent (1547): DS 1604). "Sacramental grace" is the grace of the Holy Spirit, given by Christ and proper to each sacrament. The Spirit heals and transforms those who receive him by conforming them to the Son of God. The fruit of the sacramental life is that the Spirit of adoption makes faithful partakers in the divine nature (cf. 2 Pet 1:4) by uniting them in a living union with the only Son, the Savior. —Catechism of the Catholic Church, 1129

The sacraments of the Church were given to us by Jesus Himself to unite us to His divine nature and, thus, help us in executing the plan that He has for us. As we live out the grace received in the sacraments, God is by our side with the indwelling of the Holy Spirit, not only leading us to everlasting salvation but inspiring us to assist others in their journey toward salvation.

God does His work in and through us. Because of this, we are all responsible, as disciples of Jesus Christ, for bringing back inactive Catholics to the Faith. This cannot be done only by deacons, priests, bishops, or religious. Each of us has a responsibility and a role to play in the salvation of the Good Shepherd's lost sheep. As Christians, we make up the Body of Christ, and each of us is endowed with special gifts, such as speech, leadership, wisdom, persuasion, love of the Faith, or, simply, unceasing prayer. Most of all, if we love God with all our hearts, our souls, and our minds, and give ourselves entirely to His mission, we have what it takes to be disciples of Christ who personally reach out to inactive Catholics to start them back on the road to salvation. All it really takes is a deep desire and a love of God and our neighbor.

In the Gospel of St. Luke, Jesus explains the importance of this mission in the Parable of the Lost Sheep:

> *"What man among you having a hundred sheep and losing one of them would not leave the ninety-nine in the desert and go after the lost one until he finds it? And when he does find it, he sets it on his shoulders with great joy*

and, upon arrival home, he calls together his friends and neighbors and says to them, 'Rejoice with me because I have found my lost sheep.'"

—Luke 15:3–6

What follows in the chapters of this book is the story of God calling me to The Mission of the Seventy-Two, an example of how God's love has transformed my life in ways I never imagined possible, and how His plan has given me the courage to fully accept the gift of discipleship. What is the Lord asking of you? Would you recognize His voice? What might you gain by allowing Him to lead your life?

Chapter 1

It Takes One to Know One

In January of 1985, I lost my best friend, Kevin, to a tragic car accident. He was only twenty-seven years old when he died, and I was devastated. Growing up, we had done pretty much everything together. He was not only a big part of my life, but he was family. My mother called him her second son, and I considered him a brother. At his funeral, I prayed for Kevin's soul while attending Mass with my family. Although I wondered why Kevin had to leave this world at such an early age, I didn't really blame God for his death because I knew I would meet him again someday in Heaven. I believed that the cause of his death was something that happened in this world and wasn't directed from God. I just knew I had lost my best friend, and I would have a big void in my life.

In the fall of 1984, just prior to Kevin's accident, my mother, JoAnn, was diagnosed with breast cancer and needed surgery. She was also devastated by the loss of Kevin as she was fighting her own battle against cancer. She struggled throughout that year as the cancer returned following her surgery and countless chemotherapy sessions. Although she still had hope that she could beat the cancer that was beginning to ravage her body, she faced the possibility that she might join Kevin and the faithful in Heaven. My mother loved God and her Faith, and she still remains my role model as I journey in my own faith.

In the summer of 1985, my mother wrote a letter to my father that included a section for my sister, Brenda, and me:

> You both have all the necessary tools to accomplish whatever you set out to do. Please continue to set goals and search for that dream. Believe in yourselves. You are both kind, considerate, and loving. These are wonderful qualities and someone will discover that too, and then your life will be fulfilled with someone to share your lives with as I was lucky enough to share with someone as your father [sic].

In November of 1985, my mother and I were able to attend the Iowa vs. Ohio State game so she could be present to watch her beloved Buckeyes. She struggled that day because the cancer had made its way to her lungs, and she had great difficulty breathing. A week later, when she was admitted to the hospital, the doctors told us that there was nothing else they could do for her. Upon hearing this, my mother said that all she wanted was to go home and sit in her recliner. We were fortunate to get her home so she could do just that, and she passed away a couple of hours later. My mother was only forty-nine years old when the Lord ushered her to Heaven. I don't remember much about the funeral beyond having the biggest void in my life. I still had hope for Heaven, and I trusted that I would see my mother and Kevin one day, but I knew I would miss them terribly in this world.

Although I did not blame God for these events in my life, I stopped going to Mass regularly, and soon I did not attend at all. I felt empty inside, and other concerns in my life began to take priority. My father, Carl, occasionally attended Mass on Sundays, but it had been my mother who was the glue that held our family and our faith lives together, and, when we lost her to cancer, I lost my connection with God. I just did not feel the closeness to God that once came easily to me, and I did not feel a part of God's family or a connection to the Mass itself. I was now a lost sheep wandering aimlessly away from the Good Shepherd. As Isaiah tells us: *"We had all gone astray like sheep, all following our own way"* (Is 53:6). The void in my life and the anguish that I felt is reflected in the Psalm: *"My God, my God, why have you abandoned me? Why so far from my call for help, from my cries of anguish? My God, I call by day, but you do not answer; by night, but I have no relief"* (Ps 22:2–3).

Fortunately, all was not lost. Even though I was away from God, I still had hope for Heaven and trusted that one day, I would join my family, friends, neighbors, and the rest of God's family in Heaven. Although my sorrow kept me from fully recognizing God's love for me, even in my pain, I just needed to trust in the words that my mother gave me, and, more importantly, in God's plan for me.

The Journey Home

My cousin Jan introduced me to Gloria in 1987, and we dated a few times over the next three years without it going anywhere. However, just before Christmas of 1990, Gloria unexpectedly sent me a Christmas card, which simply read, "Merry Christmas, Gloria." I thought to myself, What a nice gesture, and decided to ask her out again. We went on a couple of dates leading up to Valentine's Day, when something special happened. It was not the special Valentine's Day dinner or the gifts we exchanged but God's hand in bringing us together. God had a plan for both of us, and His plan would include much more than dating and our eventual marriage.

Gloria was Catholic and attended Mass every Sunday. I loved that about her, and I loved that attending Sunday Mass together was a part of our relationship. She slowly drew me closer to God, more so than I had been in a very long time, and, in doing so, she brought me up from the despair and sorrow of losing both my mother and my best friend. Christ was calling me back to the Church through one of his disciples—Gloria. She showed me not by words but by her actions the way back to the Church and Mass. She didn't know that I was inactive in my faith but it didn't make any difference because her faith was strong enough for both of us. Gloria did not know that she brought me back to the Faith until just a couple of years ago when I told her my story.

What came to me recently are the first verses of the hymn "Amazing Grace": "Amazing Grace! How sweet the sound, that saved a wretch like me! I once was lost, but now am found, was blind, but now I see." Gloria was responsible for my journey to discipleship and drawing me closer to God, and I'm so thankful that she was a faithful disciple of Christ who led me back to the Church.

In March of 1991, just a few weeks after our first Valentine's Day, I asked Gloria to marry me, and she said yes. God knew of this proposal long before it took place—He had plans for Gloria and me.

My mother had always held onto the hope that I would share my life with someone, and this was also part of God's plan, but I soon came to realize that His plan went much further than just a fulfilling relationship or marriage. God's plan had a purpose that involved my future wife. He called Gloria to do His will in a way that neither of us might have imagined—and it was through Gloria that Christ the Good Shepherd brought me, one of His lost sheep, back into His fold. St. Paul tells us in Romans, Chapter 8: *"We know that all things work for good for those who love God, who are called according to his purpose. For those he foreknew he also pre-destined to be conformed to the image of his Son, so that he might be the firstborn among many brothers"* (v. 29).

God's plan for me included marriage to Gloria, and we were married on March 7, 1992 by Fr. Carmen Arcuri at St. Paul's Catholic Church, the parish where my parents were married, and the parish where I grew up and had spent all of my life. Through the Sacrament of Matrimony, we were now one with each other and with God, Who would be in us in a new way, and we in Him. Through God's grace as a couple, our love would grow for each other, for Him, and for our family. As the Catechism tells us:

> "By reason of their state in life and of their order, [Christian spouses] have their own special gifts in the people of God" (*LG*, 11§ 2). This grace proper to the sacrament of Matrimony is intended to perfect the couple's love and to strengthen their indissoluble unity. By this grace they "help one another to attain holiness in their married life and in welcoming and educating children" (*LG*, 11§ 2; *cf. LG*, 41).

—*Catechism of the Catholic Church,* 1641

The Eucharist has always been an integral part of my life, and Gloria and I chose the Wedding at Cana for the Gospel reading at our wedding because that is where Jesus performed His first miracle. When the wine ran out at the Wedding at Cana, Jesus turned the stone jars of water into the very best wine, foreshadowing the Last Supper when He would change bread and wine into His very own Body and Blood. Many years later, Gloria and I would go on a pilgrimage to the Holy Land where we would renew our wedding vows in Cana where Jesus performed the first miracle of His ministry.

One of the most important aspects of marriage is that it not only encompasses the sharing of love for one another, but it is built on sacrifice. Each spouse sacrifices for the other and assists in bringing his or her spouse closer to salvation. Husband and wife take on the mission of the Church by helping each other and making sacrifices for each other. Within the Sacrament of Matrimony, spouses work to bring each other, and their children and family members, to Heaven to spend eternity with God.

Gloria and I would soon have a daughter, Sophia, born in 1994, and a son, Carl William, born in 1995. Like their father, they were both baptized at St. Paul's Catholic Church; one generation following another being baptized into the Catholic Faith. We attended Mass as a family at St. Paul's, where Gloria and I were involved in parish life, and where a good friend of mine, Mickey Hawkins, was an ordained deacon. As I watched him assisting at some of the Masses, I thought to myself, what a wonderful way of serving the Lord; I wonder if I could ever be ordained as a deacon. I did not know it at the time, but God was mapping out His plan for me by planting a seed of faith within me.

A Vocation to the Diaconate

Gloria and I lived just two miles from St. John Neumann Parish in Sunbury, Ohio, so we decided to transfer there. This, of course, was also a part of God's plan for us and for what He wanted to accomplish through us. When we walked through the doors of St. John Neumann for the first time, we felt welcomed and loved. I immediately started to get involved in parish life and became an Extraordinary Minister of Holy Communion and a member of the Finance Committee, and we volunteered as a family at some of the social events. We enrolled Sophia and Carl William in the parish school of religion and volunteered as teachers. About a year later, I signed up for an hour of Eucharistic Adoration each week. I had never experienced or knew anything at all about this devotion. I just thought that it would be a great experience to spend an hour in the presence of Our Lord. Little did I know how much that hour with Our Lord would impact my life in the years to come—all a part of God's plan for me. In speaking about time spent in Eucharistic Adoration, Pope St. John Paul II said:

> It is pleasant to spend time with Him, to lie close to His breast like the Beloved Disciple (cf. Jn 13:25) and feel the infinite love present in His heart.... How can we not feel a renewed need to spend time in spiritual converse, in silent adoration, in heartfelt love before Christ present in the Most Holy Sacrament?

> —*Ecclesia de Eucharistia*, 26

One of the personal aspects of St. John Neumann's life that I learned from a parishioner a few years after I began the devotion of Eucharistic Adoration is that he began a Forty Hours' Devotion of the Blessed Sacrament in his diocese of Philadelphia, where he was ordained bishop in 1852.

Even though I was heavily involved in parish life and several ministries at St. John Neumann, I felt a strong call from God and a deep desire in my heart to serve Him more, in a special way, but I didn't know exactly what or how I could do that. One day, unexpectedly, Gloria asked me, "Have you ever thought about becoming a deacon?" I was surprised by her question but I told her what my thoughts were when I first witnessed Deacon Mickey Hawkins during Mass at St. Paul's and confessed that, yes, I had thought about becoming a deacon and was discerning that possibility. Soon after, I began to look into the process and inquire about the vocation of becoming a deacon.

After receiving initial approval from my pastor, Fr. James Walter, in 2004, I began the application process to become a candidate to the diaconate. I was fairly far along in the process, and close to the time when the selection of candidates would occur, when Fr. Walter was transferred to another parish. Fr. David Sizemore, who was assigned as the new pastor of St. John Neumann Parish, gave me his approval and said that he would support me if I was approved as a candidate. However, I still had to receive the approval of the selection committee.

Selection letters were mailed to applicants in November every four years, and I anxiously waited for a letter from the bishop to arrive in the mail confirming my selection as a candidate. I was filled with so much joy and happiness when my letter arrived saying that I had been selected to be a candidate for the Diocese of Columbus, but, at the same time, I was anxious about what was to come.

The next three years of diaconate formation were filled with classes every other weekend, exams to take, and papers to write—quite a challenge for a husband and father who had graduated from college twenty-two years prior! However, I was not alone in my struggle because I was going through formation with fourteen brothers in Christ. I was growing in my faith through the classes and growing closer to God in learning how to administer the sacraments. I also was a part of the staff at St. John Neumann and a master of ceremonies at Masses. I frequently spoke to children in their religious education classes, was involved in all aspects of parish life, and served an internship at a neighboring parish.

One of the charisms or aspects of the ministry of a deacon is charity. I assisted with the St. Vincent de Paul Society and the Good Samaritan Ministry in serving the poor in monetary or spiritual means. This came naturally for me because I recalled and took to heart how my grandfather, Joseph Calcara, and my father, Carl Calcara, were such giving people and would do anything for someone in need. My studies and activity in parish life were part of my journey of faith and part of God's plan for me. I had a great deal of support during the years of my formation, especially from my wife, children, friends, and neighbors, and from Fr. Sizemore and all of the St. John Neumann parish community. However, I felt a void in my heart because my mother was not there for this part of my faith journey, and also because my father was in a nursing home suffering from Alzheimer's disease. Fortunately, during my formation, I learned of my spiritual mother, Mary, the Holy and Blessed Virgin Mother of Jesus. I came to recognize that she was with me, and I could go to her in prayer when I needed her most. I took to heart the Gospel passage where Jesus gave us His mother when He was dying on the Cross. As we read in the Gospel of St. John: *"When Jesus saw his mother and the disciple there whom he loved, he said to his mother, 'Woman, behold, your son.' Then he said to the disciple, 'Behold, your mother.' And from that hour the disciple took her into his home"* (Jn 19:26–27). From that moment, I began to have my mother, Mary, my spiritual mother in Heaven, pray with me and for me, interceding to her Son on my behalf. I felt that I could go to her any time I needed her support or intercession or just to feel the love of my mother in Heaven. This gave me much consolation and strength in my journey forward in this life.

As I was nearing the end of my three years of formation in the diaconate, my father finally succumbed to Alzheimer's disease and passed away. I was sad but took consolation in the fact that he was no longer suffering and was joining God and my mother in Heaven. He was the most kind and loving man I will ever know. He did not demonstrate his feelings in an outward fashion, but they were there, concealed in his heart and soul. A wise man told me at the time of my father's death that God called him to Heaven because He knew I could make the rest of my journey on my own. I hope to see my father and my mother in Heaven one day when my journey and mission is completed in this world.

On November 29, 2008, I was called to Holy Orders and ordained to the permanent diaconate at St. Joseph Cathedral in Columbus, Ohio, by the Most Rev. James A. Griffin, J.D., J.C.L. On that day, the bishop laid hands on me and my fourteen brothers just as the Apostles did when they prayed and laid hands on the first deacons of the Church, which included St.

Stephen, the first martyr of the Christian Church.

The Acts of the Apostles tells us that the Hellenists, or Greeks, complained against the Hebrews, or Jews, that their widows were being neglected in the daily distribution. Reputable men were called by the Apostles because they did not want to see the Word of God neglected to serve at table. On the day of my ordination, I was given the task of proclaiming and living the Gospel of Jesus Christ, serving at Our Lord's table in the distribution of Holy Communion, and becoming Christ the Servant to be a servant to His people.

As a deacon, I began my formal service to God's people. I would become a servant of God's Church and, in a very intimate way, a servant to all in the Church's mission of the salvation of souls. As we read in the Gospel of St. Mark:

> *"Whoever wishes to be great among you will be your servant; whoever wishes to be first among you will be the slave of all. For the Son of Man did not come to be served but to serve and to give his life as a ransom for many"* (Mk 10:43–45).

I would find out in about seven years how God wanted me to serve Him in an even more special way, a way that I could not even imagine.

Chapter 2

God's Request:

The Mission of the Seventy-Two

About seven years after my ordination to the diaconate, I went on a parish-sponsored trip to assist at a Papal Mass in Philadelphia on September 27, 2015. On the first day, we made a stop at St. Peter the Apostle Catholic Church, where the National Shrine of St. John Neumann is located, and where his incorrupt body lies beneath the altar. St. John Neumann was known for founding numerous schools, establishing at least one order of nuns, and tending to those in need, and it was such a privilege to assist at Mass there.

On Sunday, deacons from all over the United States assisted at the Papal Mass celebrated by Pope Francis at the Cathedral of the Basilica of Sts. Peter and Paul on Logan Square in Philadelphia. The deacons assisting at the Mass went out on the square to distribute Holy Communion to the thousands of Catholics in attendance. When Mass was finished, we all headed back to our buses for the ride home. This was truly a remarkable trip—to have had the opportunity to assist, not only at the church of our own parish's namesake, but also at the Most Sacred Liturgy of the Mass celebrated by the Holy Father, Pope Francis. I was delighted and filled with happiness and joy, yet I had no idea what was waiting for me just around the bend.

A few days after our return from Philadelphia, on September 29, I was leading a Eucharistic Adoration Holy Hour at our parish. As I finished praying the Evening Prayer and was sitting in the pew meditating in God's presence with my mind focused on Jesus, God came to me, and I heard Him say,

> *"I want you to go out into the homes by twos and personally reach out to inactive Catholics. Proclaim the Gospel and tell them that the Kingdom of God is at hand. Do not be afraid because I am with you."*

I went home and pondered what God had said to me and what He was asking me to do. The next evening, I was having dinner with Gloria and told her about my experience of God speaking to me in Adoration. I asked her, "Was that truly God coming to me, or was it my own thoughts?"

She replied, "You have Adoration tomorrow morning. See if God comes to you again."

The next morning, on October 1, while praying in Adoration, I didn't hear anything from God, so, as I do every day, I opened to the Scripture readings of the day, and this is what I read from the Gospel of St. Luke:

The Mission of the Seventy-Two

After this the Lord appointed seventy[-two]
others whom he sent ahead of him in pairs to
every town and place he intended to visit. He
said to them, "The harvest is abundant but
the laborers are few; so ask the master of the
harvest to send out laborers for his harvest.
Go on your way; behold, I am sending you like
lambs among wolves. Carry no money bag, no
sack, no sandals; and greet no one along the
way. Into whatever house you enter, first say,
'Peace to this household.' If a peaceful person
lives there, your peace will rest on him; but if
not, it will return to you. Stay in the same house
and eat and drink what is offered to you, for
the laborer deserves his payment. Do not move
about from one house to another. Whatever
town you enter and they welcome you, eat what
is set before you, cure the sick in it and say to
them, 'The kingdom of God is at hand for you.'"

—Luke 10:1–9

About a month after receiving this mission from God, I
spoke with Fr. Sizemore who challenged me to write up a
proposal for the ministry. I gladly accepted the challenge and,
over the next year, began to write out a description of the
ministry under the influence of the Holy Spirit, and entirely
during my time spent in Eucharistic Adoration. I knew that
if God had come to me with this mission, then He would be

at my side and the Holy Spirit would guide my thoughts and heart in writing out His mission and ministry.

Soon after I first spoke with Fr. Sizemore about receiving my mission from God, a parishioner from St. John Neumann approached me with an experience he wanted to tell me about. The parishioner had gone on a business trip to Arkansas. During dinner one evening, he struck up a conversation with a gentleman from Philadelphia. The gentleman mentioned to the parishioner that he had attended some events during the Pope's visit and had taken several photos, including photos of the Papal Mass. He showed our parishioner the photos of the Mass and, to the amazement of our parishioner, they were of me distributing communion in Logan Square.

Deacon Carl Calcara distributing Holy Communion
at the Papal Mass in Philadelphia, September 27, 2015.

Coincidence? Or a Holy Spirit-filled experience in conjunction with The Mission of the Seventy-Two? This is only one instance of the grace of the Holy Spirit working in my life in conjunction with the sacraments, The Mission of the Seventy-Two, and the Church's mission of the salvation of souls. As we read in the Catechism:

> Grace is first and foremost the gift of the Spirit who justifies and sanctifies us. But grace also includes the gifts that the Spirit grants us to associate us with his works, to enable us to collaborate in the salvation of others and in the growth of the Body of Christ, the Church.
> —*Catechism of the Catholic Church*, 2003

I continued writing out the ministry for The Mission of the Seventy-Two from the spring of 2016 through the spring of 2017. Just as I was finishing, however, Fr. Sizemore was transferred to St. Francis de Sales in Newark, and Fr. Paul Noble became the new pastor of St. John Neumann Parish. I was filled with some doubt and apprehension as to whether Fr. Noble would support me with The Mission of the Seventy-Two ministry. But, as I knew from past experiences in my life and my relationship with the Lord; God knew of His plan for me. I just needed to trust in His plan for the mission. Fr. Noble read over the ministry proposal and, in the fall of 2017, he gave me his blessing to continue with The Mission of the Seventy-Two.

As I began to organize the ministry of The Mission of the Seventy-Two, recalling the Scripture passage that God placed before me during Adoration, I thought I should research where the Catholic Church was in terms of weekly Mass attendance. I found it remarkable that the number of Catholics attending Sunday Mass in the United States in 1970 was 54.9%, while only 29% of Catholics attended Mass in 2012. Mass attendance had dropped drastically in little more than forty years. Clearly, during these four decades, there was a societal shift in which Catholics were increasingly not making Sunday Mass a priority in their lives, and there was an urgent need to reach out to inactive Catholics.

What came to my mind and heart is that God wants discipleship to be personal. As the Scripture tells us, Jesus appointed seventy-two disciples, i.e., these disciples were chosen by Jesus Himself. In a similar manner, the disciples for The Mission of the Seventy-Two ministry would be chosen by the pastor and evangelization team of St. John Neumann. They would need to be steadfast in their faith, people who had traveled on the road to discipleship themselves and who had the heart and desire to go out into the world to bring back the lost sheep of the Body of Christ. These disciples would need to be committed heart and soul to give their time freely and without reservation to reach out to inactive Catholics and let them know that they are loved and that they are missed.

When Jesus sent out the seventy-two disciples, they walked along the roads, personally knocking on doors as they went. Although the disciples of this modern-day ministry would utilize modern technology, they would still reach out and make phone calls personally to inactive Catholics. During these calls, the disciples would introduce themselves, saying hello and asking the inactive parishioners how they were doing. They would then ask about their experience at St. John Neumann and let them know about some ministry or event going on at the parish. These might be events of a particular liturgical season such as a Lenten fish fry, Stations of the Cross, or Eucharistic Adoration. They would then ask them if they had a special prayer intention that they could pray for them. The disciples would end the conversation by letting them know how good it was to speak with them, and ask God to bless them and their family. Messages would be left if the call was directed to voicemail, and, in some cases, follow-up emails would be sent. All inactive parishioners would receive a package in the mail that included a pocket book of the gospels with a message from Pope Francis saying:

> TAKE IT, CARRY IT with you, and read it every day: it is Jesus Himself who is speaking to you. . . . The important thing is to read the Word of God, by any means, but read the Word of God. It is Jesus who speaks to us there. And welcome it with an open heart. Then the good seed will bear fruit!
>
> —*Pocket Gospels and Acts of the Apostles*,
>
> Distributed by United States Conference of Catholic Bishops

The disciples would also mail a current bulletin and a magnet with scenic artwork with the parish's address, phone number, website address, Facebook address, Mass times, and where to go to live-stream Masses. Business cards would also be included in case they had any questions. Each packet would be personalized with a handwritten card in which God might speak to the inactive parishioners through His disciples. The card would reiterate the conversation with the parishioners, or just say hello and update them on what was happening at St. John Neumann Parish. The card would remind them that we were praying for them, and ask for God's blessing on them and their family. This packet would let the parishioners know in a personal way that we loved and missed them, without being judgmental about their decision not to attend Mass.

So far, the disciples have made hundreds of calls and have not been turned away, spoken to in a rude manner, or hung up on. Of the many packages that have been mailed, only one has been refused.

In this manner, The Mission of the Seventy-Two ministry would follow in the footsteps of St. Francis de Sales, who just happened to be the patron saint of the Diocese of Columbus and of the high school I attended. At the very end of the seventeenth century, at the height of the Protestant Reformation, St. Francis de Sales set out on foot with a few companions to Chablais in Alpine, France. When they arrived at their destination, they found the churches in ruin and disarray, and empty of parishioners, but for a few souls. So St. Francis began his quest by proclaiming and preaching the Gospel of the Catholic Faith. He made his plea personal and intimate, taking a gentle approach by placing either handwritten or printed pamphlets under the doors of fallen-away Catholics.

As history attests, this "gentle" approach of St. Francis de Sales bore much fruit. In just four years, and after forty hours of Eucharistic Adoration held in the capital city of Thonon, Chablais, he and just a few companions called between 40,000 to 72,000 former Catholics back to the Church.

When I finished the ministry proposal, and we started to make the first calls and send out the first packets in the fall of 2017, I thought I had completed what God had asked me to do. I should have known better! God had other plans. He placed a disciple in my path who would allow me to reach out to thousands of inactive Catholics. This second part of God's plan would create an abundance of disciples. This sounds impossible, right? Just remember: all things are possible with God.

๑   ๑

Chapter 3

Empowering Active Catholics

I was just beginning to recruit disciples for the new ministry of The Mission of the Seventy-Two in the fall of 2017 when one of our parishioners, Steve, suggested that it would be great if we could put something in the hands of parishioners to empower them to reach out to their families, friends, neighbors, fellow parishioners, and even strangers to invite them back to the Church. This approach might potentially reach thousands of inactive Catholics by giving active Catholics the tools they needed to be true disciples. Just imagine if all active parishioners in the Catholic Church were empowered to reach out to the lost sheep of the Church. The possibilities would be endless, and the impossibilities would become possible. The faithful could reach out to the ones they loved in a very intimate and personal way, showing the lost ones how much they are missed at Mass by both God and their own family members.

I gave much thought and prayer to this idea and was inspired by the Holy Spirit to begin the far-reaching aspect of this Mission. I utilized my holy hours of Eucharistic Adoration to be inspired by God Himself and influenced by the Holy Spirit to write out a card that could be put in the hands of active disciples offering suggestions for reaching out to inactive family, friends, neighbors, and fellow parishioners.

There are three aspects to the card: prayer, preparation, and action. On one side of the card is the Divine Mercy image of Christ displaying His Divine Mercy and love streaming from His Sacred Heart. Then, the perfect prayer from the Divine Mercy Chaplet Novena prayer that Jesus gave to Sr. Faustina. We must pray this Novena prayer unceasingly for our brothers and sisters in Christ separated from the Church I will elaborate more on praying for Inactive Catholics in Chapter 5.

Before reaching out to inactive Catholics, we must prepare ourselves to be a beacon of God's Love and Mercy. We must prepare as a soldier going into battle; only, we are preparing to put on the armor of Christ going against the evil one who has captured the souls of our loved ones. We must ask the Holy Spirit to come upon us, prepare us, and do a *JIG*.

*J*oy-filled life we live in God. Find and share the joy you have in living your Catholic faith having a personal relationship with Jesus. Let this take center stage in your own heart and soul with the hope God will use it to draw others close to Him and you.

*I*nvest in relationships with those you want to bring back to the faith and to Mass. This investment includes prayer and doing activities that strengthen your relationship with the ones you love. Whatever you do together doesn't have to directly involve faith. Simply spending time together may be the sacrificial gift a person needs.

*G*et curious why your family, friends, or neighbors may have abandoned their faith and stopped coming to Mass. Do not assume you know all the answers. Gently, and with love, ask questions without your emotions getting away from you.

Don't be afraid to start the conversation about attending Mass.

After doing a *JIG*, you are ready to take a *LEAP* of Faith to do battle for the souls of your loved ones. In taking this *LEAP* of Faith, you are trusting in Jesus that He will give you a loving heart for His Mission.

*L*isten to where they may be with their faith journey. Pray to God that He will give you the ears to hear and the heart to listen. This step must not be rushed and needs to be done with patience and without judgment.

*E*xtend your love; be the light of Christ extending God's mercy working in and through you. Let your family, friends, or neighbors know God loves them and they are missed at Mass. Share why you love the Mass and what it means to you.

*A*ttend to their misgivings, excuses and doubts about their faith. Find the answers to their misgivings, the guidance to their excuses, and truths to their doubts. Use your God-given wisdom coming from your mind and heart; this wisdom will be sufficient enough.

*P*ray to have courage and love for your family, friends, or neighbors to invite them back to the Church. Personally extend the invitation to attend Mass with you. Plan to meet at the doors of the Church to prove you will be at their side on their journey. If the invitation is declined, give it some time before trying again. God never gives up on us; we should never give up on our loved ones and friends.

These three steps of prayer, preparation, and action may take some time, but we must remember: everything happens in God's time and not in ours. Inactive Catholics did not leave the Church overnight; they will not come back overnight. The Trinity lives within us so we need not be afraid; God is with us at all times!

We have prepared this day to do battle against the evil one for the salvation of souls; we must not fail!

Let the Blessing of Almighty God be with us on the greatest Mission of our time: the salvation of souls.

Chapter 4

The Importance of the Sacraments in the Life of a Disciple

The Sacrament of Baptism

G od knows each of us and has a plan for us, even before we are conceived. As we read in the Psalms:

> *You formed my inmost being: you knit me in my mother's womb. I praise you, so wonderfully you made me; wonderful are your works! My very self you knew; my bones were not hidden from you, When I was being made in secret, fashioned as in the depths of the earth. Your eyes foresaw my actions; in your book all are written down; my days shaped, before one came to be.*
>
> —Psalm 139:13–17

Later, in the New Testament, when Jesus established His kingdom and unveiled His plan of salvation, He stressed the essential nature of Baptism. Speaking to Nicodemus, He explained how it was possible for a man to be born again:

"Amen, amen, I say to you, no one can enter the kingdom of God without being of water and the Spirit" (Jn 3:5). And St. Paul further elaborated on the importance of Baptism in his Letter to the Romans:

> *Or are you unaware that we who were bap-tized into Christ Jesus were baptized into his death? We were indeed buried with him through baptism into death, so that, just as Christ was raised from the dead by the glory of the Father, we too might live in the new-ness of life. For if we have grown into union with him through death like his, we shall also be united with him in the resurrection."*

—Romans 6:3–5

In the Church's Rite for the Order of Baptism of Children, when the parents state that they want Baptism for their child, the celebrant says: "In asking for Baptism for your child, you are undertaking the responsibility of raising him (her) in the faith, so that, keeping God's commandments, he (she) may love the Lord and his (her) neighbor as Christ has taught us. Do you understand this responsibility?" The parents answer with: "We do." Then the godparents are asked: "Are you ready to help the parents of this child in their duty?" The godparents answer, "We are (I am)."

Parents who are living out God's plan listen to the words of Christ and become willing participants in His plan by bringing their children to the Sacrament of Baptism. They understand that their children are gifts from God and that through the Sacrament of Baptism their children become God's children and join His community of believers, and they readily accept their responsibility of raising their children in the Faith.

However, even though God had a plan for us before we were conceived, we as human beings have a free will and can deviate from His plans. For example, some parents, not knowing God at all or being away from God and the Faith, do not bring their children to the Sacrament of Baptism. In these cases, it is our responsibility as disciples, as Christians, and as witnesses to the Faith to assist and reach out to them regarding the importance of bringing their children to the sacrament. However, it is equally important to remember that our responsibility as disciples of Christ extends well past the Baptism of their children.

You may have heard that it takes a village to raise a child. Well, it also takes the whole Church community to raise a child in the Faith. Just as the secular community shares a responsibility in the education and upbringing of a child in life, the Church community shares a responsibility in raising a child in the Faith. When our children become adults, they venture out into the world because they have all of the necessary tools to take on the world. Likewise, when our children, through the Sacrament of Baptism, are raised in the Faith by the community of believers, they should be ready to go out into the world to be steadfast witnesses to their Faith. Just as children are nurtured by their parents and others to succeed in the world, the children of God's community should have walked hand in hand with the community of believers to become faithful adult members of the Body of Christ.

Unfortunately, there is sometimes a breakdown with the parents, or godparents, or the Church community in raising children in the Faith (including those coming into the Faith through Rite of Christian Initiation) in that when they go out into the world they are influenced or swayed by what the world has to offer them. The world envelopes their hearts and souls to make the priorities of the world their priorities, and, subsequently, the Faith becomes a lower priority in their lives. When children or new Catholics reject or lose their faith, the community of believers must make it their priority to bring them back to the Church and their faith.

St. Paul sets an example for us when he personally returned to Corinth, or sent his disciples there, on three different occasions because the newly baptized had turned away from their faith. These new Christians, who had become prideful and selfish, reverted to their former practice of paganism, began to follow false apostles, or were just being influenced by what was going on in their society at that time. St. Paul understood that it was of the utmost importance to return to Corinth to bring these newly baptized Christians back to their faith in Jesus Christ, no matter how much of his time it took, or how many times he needed to return.

We, of course, live in a different time, but we face many of the same issues and influences that these early Christians faced. And, although our world may be quite different, we encounter the same challenge as St. Paul in that many baptized Catholics have separated themselves from the Body of Christ—Christ's Church. Just as St. Paul reached out to the community of believers in Corinth, we too need to personally reach out to inactive Catholics and invite them back to the Church. By word and action, and by being witnesses to the Faith, we need to step up as a community of believers in seeking out the lost ones who were baptized into the Faith.

In reaching out to inactive Catholics, however, we must draw upon the sanctifying grace that we first received in Baptism, for without union with Christ and reliance on His graces, we would be entirely ineffective in sharing Christ's love with others.

> "'Reborn as sons of God, [the baptized] must profess before men the faith they have received from God through the Church' and participate in the apostolic and missionary activity of the People of God" (*LG*, 11; *cf. LG*, 17; *AG*, 7; 23).
> —*Catechism of the Catholic Church*, 1270

As active Catholics filled with God's grace, we need to profess our love for God, our Faith, and our neighbors, both in word and action, so that the lost ones will see how much we love God and love them, and they will want what we have and come back to the Church.

The Sacrament of Confirmation

The incredible graces that we first received in Baptism, which enable us to be witnesses for Christ, are further strengthened in the Sacrament of Confirmation when we receive an outpouring of the Holy Spirit. The graces that we receive in Confirmation enable us to become more fully engaged in the salvific mission of the Church for the salvation of souls and give us strength to more fully participate in God's plan. Through Confirmation, we become more like Christ and can draw from Him the strength we need to go out into the world to be witnesses to the Faith by word and deed. Anointed with Sacred Chrism, we are empowered to be soldiers in Christ's army, defending Christ and the Church through our witness to the Catholic Faith. We are strengthened to fight battles for the Lord by standing up for the Catholic Faith and opposing evil in the world. As we read in Ephesians:

> *Finally, draw your strength from the Lord and from his mighty power. Put on the armor of God so that you may be able to stand against the tactics of the devil. For our struggle is not flesh and blood but the principalities, with the powers, with the world rulers of this present darkness, with the evil spirits in the heavens. Therefore, put on the armor of God, that you may be able to resist on the evil day and, having done everything, to hold your ground. So stand fast with your loins girded in truth, clothed with righteousness as a breastplate, and your feet shod in readiness for the gospel*

*of peace. In all circumstances, hold faith as a
shield, to quench all [the] flaming arrows of the
evil one. And take the helmet of salvation and
sword of the Spirit, which is the word of God.*

—Ephesians 6:10–17

Through the Sacrament of Confirmation, we are made soldiers of Christ and given the grace and strength to fully participate in the mission of the salvation of souls by personally reaching out to inactive Catholics who have been captured by the world. Over the last couple of centuries, American soldiers have fought bravely and courageously for life, liberty, and the pursuit of happiness. They have fought for their country in battles all over the world, sometimes making the ultimate sacrifice of giving their lives courageously for others. Likewise, soldiers of Christ stand up for the way, the truth, and the life, and are counted as Christians in the Faith for the salvation of lost souls.

Active Catholics need to remember the supreme sacrifice that Christ made for all by dying on the Cross so that we could share in the eternal life of Heaven. Active Catholics need not be afraid and should put feelings aside and express only sacrificial love in bringing inactive Catholics back to the Church. As soldiers of Christ, we are losing many battles in bringing those lost to the Faith back to the Church, but we know who wins the war with the Second Coming of Christ. As active members of the Church, we must seize the day and begin to personally reach out to inactive Catholics no matter how many times or how long it takes to win them back.

The Liturgy of the Mass

Growing up, I always understood the importance of attending Sunday Mass primarily because of the Third Commandment, which instructs us to worship the Lord on Sundays.

> *Remember the Sabbath day—keep it holy. Six days you may labor and do all your work, but the seventh day is a Sabbath of the Lord your God. You shall not do any work, either you, son or your daughter, your male or female slave, your work animal, or the resident alien within your gates. For in six days the Lord made the heavens and the earth, the sea and all that is in them, but on the seventh day he rested. That is why the Lord has blessed the sabbath day and made it holy.*

—Exodus 20:8–11

I also understood that Sunday was supposed to be a day of rest because God rested on the seventh day of creation. While I knew that Mass was a serious obligation, I never really understood in a meaningful way what the Mass was about or what it should mean to me as a Catholic. I loved receiving Holy Communion but didn't really understand the readings, why we sang hymns or repeated various prayers, or even the importance of the Mass and how the Mass originated. Now, as a deacon of the Church, I have had the opportunity to study the Mass and understand why it is important in the Christian life. As Catholics, we come together to celebrate God's Most Sacred Liturgy of the Mass, where we hear God's Word proclaimed and share in the Eucharist in God's holy banquet at His altar. I also understand why it is important to come together as a community of believers; and why, after we hear God's Word and are fed at His heavenly banquet here on earth, we are sent forth to proclaim His Word and by our actions bring Christ to the world.

But what about our children or even adults who have not been catechized properly? Could this be one reason why the Church is losing over fifty percent of her children who, by the time they reach the age of twenty-three, stop practicing the Faith? The Church is losing her children, God's children, the future Church, to the world.

When we speak to inactive Catholics about why they don't attend Mass, we receive a wide variety of answers: I receive God in nature; I pray on my own; the Mass is boring; I don't understand the Mass; someone from the Church treated me badly or yelled at me; I don't like the music; I don't like all the kneeling and standing; the Mass is too long; and many other reasons and excuses. Because of this, we need to educate our children, parents, brothers and sisters, aunts and uncles, and all members of the Church on the true meaning and importance of the Mass. We should be able to explain to others why we sing, stand, and kneel, and the meaning of God's Word (the readings), the homily, the Prayers of the Faithful, the Offertory, the Eucharistic Prayers, the Creed, and the different prayers of the Mass, including the Lord's Prayer, Holy Communion, the Closing Prayer, and being sent forth at the end of Mass. Every parish in the world should educate its parishioners on what the Mass is about and what the Mass means to them. There are many good books, DVDs, and adult formation classes on the Mass that should be offered at every parish, and the parts of the Mass should be carefully explained each year to our students in religious education classes in our Catholic schools and parishes. When children and their parents understand and love the Mass, it greatly increases the probability that they will stay on the road to salvation. And, when the children stay in their Faith, it ensures the future of the Church for decades and centuries to come.

Parents should encourage their children at a very young age to get involved in the Mass. They can become altar servers, most of the time, when they are in the third or fourth grade. When they receive the Sacrament of Confirmation, they can become lectors or Extraordinary Ministers of Holy Communion. They can also sing or play an instrument in the choir or band, or become greeters or ushers to meet parishioners when they come through the doors of the Church. One young boy at our parish couldn't wait to tell me he was going to be a greeter. We should also encourage our children to volunteer in some capacity with the Church or some service organization associated with the Church like a soup kitchen or other non-profits associated directly or indirectly with the Church. The generation that volunteered in the Church is being ushered into Heaven, meaning there will be fewer servants to sustain the Church in the future.

If our children better understand the Mass and what it means to them, and are involved with God's Most Sacred Liturgy, then the Church has a better opportunity to keep them engaged in their Faith. This also instills in them the service of volunteering, which is vitally important for the future Church. When our children step up and are regarded as servants of Christ, they will be a shining example to their peers.

As disciples, we need to stress the importance of immersing our children in God's Most Sacred Liturgy so they understand the significance of the Mass and, more importantly, why it is important in their lives. We have to help them understand that the Mass is more than an obligation, it is life in God, and it is at Mass when we experience Heaven on earth. We need to teach our children that keeping the Sabbath is all about worshiping God and passing on their Faith to their children. While this is not the only answer, it is important in keeping children in the Faith.

It's not only important that we educate our children about the Mass but all the faithful on what the Mass is about and what it should mean to them. We read in the Vatican II documents on the Sacred Liturgy:

> With zeal and patience pastors of souls must promote participation, both internal and external, taking into account their age, condition, way of life and standard of religious culture. By so doing pastors will be fulfilling one of the chief duties of a faithful dispenser of the mysteries of God, and in this matter they must lead their flock not only by word but also by example.

—*Sacrosanctum Concilium*, 19

It's not only the responsibility of bishops, priests, deacons, and religious to be zealous and educate the faithful (the laity) on the Mass; rather, it's the responsibility of every soul that makes up the Body of Christ. Every member of the Church must take responsibility for a family member, friend, neighbor, or fellow parishioner who doesn't understand and attend Mass. If the active members of the Church truly understand the Mass and have confidence in what the Mass is all about and what it can mean in the lives of inactive members, then they should be zealous in their pursuit of the inactive members and take the opportunity to speak to them about the Mass. These conversations, however, must always be done in a loving and inviting way, so that the inactive members do not feel they are being preached at, but instead understand that they are missed and loved. And if, after these conversations, the inactive members decide to give Mass another try, then the active members should meet them at the doors of the Church to welcome them, to walk through the doors together, and to answer any questions that they might have.

The Sacrament of the Eucharist

The Eucharist, the Sacrament of Holy Communion, has always been the source and summit of my faith. It is the common thread that runs through my life, and it is an integral part of God's plan for me. From the Eucharist, I gain strength and insight into God's plan, and He works through me and within me to bring others to salvation. Jesus stressed the importance of receiving Holy Communion when He told the crowds:

> *"Amen, Amen, I say to you, unless you eat the flesh of the Son of Man and drink his blood, you do not have life within you. Whoever eats my flesh and drinks my blood has eternal life, and I will raise him on the last day. For my flesh is true food, and my blood is true drink. Whoever eats my flesh and drinks my blood remains in me and I in him. Just as the living Father sent me and I have life because of the Father, so also the one who feeds on me will have life because of me. This is the bread that came down from heaven."*

—John 6:53–58

When Jesus spoke the preceding passage, some of His disciples could not understand what He said, and many who had been His followers left Him that day. The same is true in today's Church. A recent Pew Research Center survey reported that only 31% of practicing Catholics believe in the Real Presence of Christ in the Eucharist. This means that most practicing Catholics no longer believe that the bread and wine become the Body and Blood of Christ following the Words of Consecration. The same is even more true for inactive Catholics, most of whom do not believe in the Real Presence of Christ in the Eucharist and do not realize that the Eucharist is the source and summit of our lives. As the Catechism tells us:

There is no surer pledge or clearer sign of this great hope in the new heavens and new earth, "in which righteousness dwells" (2 *Pet* 3:13), than the Eucharist. Every time this mystery is celebrated, "the work of our redemption is carried on" and we "break the one bread that provides medicine of immortality, the antidote for death, and the food that makes us live forever in Jesus Christ" (*LG*, 3; St. Ignatius of Antioch, *Ad. Eph.* 20, 2: SCh 10, 76).

—*Catechism of the Catholic Church*, 1405

Personally, I would come to understand this Scripture passage from the Gospel of St. John in an extraordinary way later in my life when God would present before my eyes the miracle of the Eucharist in conjunction with The Mission of the Seventy-Two ministry.

The frequent reception of Holy Communion and the graces that we receive are absolutely essential for The Mission of the Seventy-Two and the sharing of our Faith with inactive Catholics. When we receive the Eucharist, we are nourished at God's table, and the graces received in Holy Communion assist us on our journey to Heaven. Because of the centrality of the Eucharist to our Faith, and the incredible graces received in Holy Communion, it is more important than ever for those of us who do believe in the Real Presence to personally share our belief with those who don't believe whenever we have the opportunity to do so, and even to go out of our way to do so.

When we consume the Body and Blood of Christ in Holy Communion, we become what we eat. And, when we receive Christ in the Eucharist, others should see Christ in us. Through the Eucharist, we are enabled to give of ourselves in charity to others in the hope that we can assist them in coming back to the Eucharist and to the Mass. What greater charity could there be than being nourished at God's table and then personally reaching out to those not attending His paschal banquet within the Mass? Christ gave us food for our journey, and it is only right that we share it with others who are without it, and need it.

The reason some Catholics come back to the Church on their own is because they yearn for the Eucharist and realize it is the source and summit of their lives, and they are living without it. This need for the Eucharist in our lives could be a conversation starter when active Catholics reach out to inactive Catholics.

The Sacrament of Reconciliation

Scripture tells us that Christ gave His authority to forgive sins to the Apostles, who then passed this authority on to their successors. "[Jesus] said to them again, 'Peace be with you. As the father has sent me, so I send you.' And when he had said this he breathed on them and said to them,

> *'Receive the Holy Spirit. Whose sins you forgive are forgiven them, and whose sins you retain are retained'"* (Jn 20:21–23).

Diaconate candidates are encouraged to go to Confession at least once a month. When I first heard this, I had much anxiety and apprehension. Like many Catholics, I had not gone to Confession very often in the last several years. There was a parish close to my workplace that offered Confessions once a week after Mass, so I thought I would give it a try. The priest was very nice and helped me to make a good Confession. After I left the confessional and did my penance, I was euphoric. My sins had been washed away, and I felt cleansed. Following this, I started to go to Confession at least once a month, or as often as I needed to receive the sacrament. Over time, I have come to love the Sacrament of Reconciliation and understand its importance in the life of a disciple. Through this sacrament, sins are forgiven, and we are left with a feeling of joy that draws us closer to God and restores our friendship with Him on our journey of faith. The Catechism tells us the importance of this sacrament when it says:

> "The whole power of the sacrament of Penance consists in restoring to God's grace and joining with him in an intimate friendship" (*Roman Catechism*, II, V, 18). Reconciliation with God is thus the purpose and effect of this sacrament. For those who receive the sacrament of Penance with contrite heart and religious disposition, reconciliation "is usually followed by peace and serenity of conscience with strong consolation" [Council of Trent (1551): DS 1674].
>
> —*Catechism of the Catholic Church*, 1468

Unfortunately, the majority of Catholics, active or inactive, do not receive the Sacrament of Reconciliation or Confession often. In fact, according to CARA (Center for Applied Research for the Apostolate), only 2% of Catholics go to Confession regularly and three quarters of Catholics never go to Confession, or go less than once a year.

As Catholics, when we confess our sins, we know that a healing takes place, a healing of heart and soul, and we have a feeling of inner peace. When we confess our sins through the Sacrament of Reconciliation, we are forgiven, and we are reconciled with God. This joy of peace and forgiveness is something that active Catholics need to pass along to inactive Catholics who have been away from the Church for some time and need to be reconciled to God through the Sacrament of Reconciliation. It should also be recommended that once they start back to Mass, and before they receive Holy Communion, that they confess their sins to God in the sacrament. You should also recommend that they talk with a priest.

Chapter 5

Praying for Inactive Catholics

The Mission of the Seventy-Two would not be possible without prayer. Disciples need to pray unceasingly for inactive Catholics. As St. Paul tells us in 1 Thessalonians:

> We urge you brothers, admonish the idle, cheer the fainthearted, support the weak, be patient with all. . . . Rejoice always. Pray without ceasing. In all circumstances give thanks, for this is the will of God for you in Christ Jesus.
>
> —1 Thessalonians 5:14, 16–18

As the preceding passage reminds us, we must be patient and trust in God when requesting answers to our prayers, especially in the ministry of inviting inactive Catholics back to the Church. Many inactive Catholics did not leave the Church overnight; instead, new habits were formed over many, many years and for a variety of reasons, often quite personal. While we can rest assured that God always answers our prayers, especially when we pray for His lost sheep, it is important to remember that our prayers are answered in God's time—not our time. We read in the Gospel of St. John:

> *"It was not you who chose me, but I chose you and appointed you to go and bear fruit that will remain, so that whatever you ask the Father in my name he may give you"* (Jn 15:16).

Jesus Himself gave us the prayer of Divine Mercy for the ministry, which I would like to suggest as the perfect prayer for calling inactive Catholics back to God's Church. This prayer is found in the fifth day of the Novena to the Divine Mercy that Jesus gave to St. Maria Faustina Kowalska entitled "Today bring to Me the souls of those who have separated themselves from the Church":

> Most Merciful Jesus, Goodness Itself, You do not refuse light to those who seek it of You. Receive into the abode of Your Most Compassionate Heart the souls of those who have separated themselves from Your Church. Draw them by Your light into the unity of the Church, and do not let them escape from the abode of Your Compassionate Heart; but bring it about that they, too, come to glorify the generosity of Your mercy.

> Eternal Father, turn Your merciful gaze upon the souls of those who have separated themselves from Your Son's Church, who have squandered Your blessings and misused Your graces by obstinately persisting in their errors. Do not look upon their errors, but upon the love of Your own Son and upon His bitter Passion, which He underwent for their sake, since they, too, are enclosed in His Most Compassionate

Heart. Bring it about that they also may glorify Your great mercy for endless ages. Amen.

—Divine Mercy Chaplet

This novena prayer can be prayed each day for all inactive Catholics who are separated from the Church. Every Saturday or Sunday, I pray the novena prayer and then pray for each inactive family at St. John Neumann Parish. On the Hail Mary beads, I pray as follows: "For the sake of His sorrowful Passion, have mercy on us and on the whole world and for the John and Mary Doe Family."

I always pray the novena in Eucharistic Adoration in the direct presence of our Lord. Active Catholics can pray any prayer or Rosary, anywhere or at any time, during the course of the day, but we must make the time each day to pray for the inactive Catholics of the Church if we are to answer God's call to be His disciples. In a special way we should pray for our adult children who do not practice or have left the Faith.

When we pray, it is normal to pray for ourselves and our needs. However, we must not embrace what prayer can do only for ourselves but what it can do for others who need our prayers the most. We should put others before ourselves when we pray, just as Jesus prayed to His Father for us in our time of need and was heard.

While we understand that having an active prayer life is good, there never seems to be enough time in the day to pray even for those who are in most need of our prayers. However, we must make the supreme sacrifice of our time with the ultimate goal of bringing back lost souls to the Church, seeing into the future when all Catholics can come together as one Body giving all praise and glory to God, praising Him in His Most Sacred Liturgy. If we really think about it, how much time in the day do we do meaningless things that we could fill with prayer, especially praying for others in need? We could take at least five to ten minutes each day to pray for those separated from the Church. And what could be more important in your day than praying for the return of a lost soul to the Church?

God will answer your prayer, but it will take your participation as one of His disciples to make the prayer happen. We must remember that an inactive Catholic did not leave the Church overnight, and it will take months, or perhaps years, before he or she comes back to the Church.

In some cases I believe we find the perfect prayer in Scripture itself—God's Word. That is exactly what I came across in St. Paul's Letter to the Romans as I was praying the Evening Prayer in the Liturgy of the Hours:

> *We who are strong ought to put up with the failings of the weak and not to please ourselves; let each of us please our neighbor for the good, for building up. For Christ did not please himself; but, as it is written, "The insults of those who insult you*

fall upon me." For whatever was written previously was written for our instruction, that by endurance and by the encouragement of the scriptures we might have hope. May the God of endurance and encouragement grant you to think in harmony with one another, in keeping with Christ Jesus, that with one accord you may with one voice glorify the God and Father of our Lord Jesus Christ.

—Romans 15:1–6

St. Monica, St. Augustine's mother, prayed unceasingly for years for her son to come back to the Church. It took many years and much patience, but she didn't give up on God or on her son. She had great confidence that He would answer her prayers and that her son would come back to the Faith—and God did answer her prayers. St. Monica is a great personal example for all of us to follow in praying for inactive Catholics to come back to the Church. We pray in our time and God answers our prayers in His time.

❦   ❧

Chapter 6

God Is with Us

Jesus, as a part of His plan of salvation, gave us His Body and Blood as spiritual food and drink to sustain us in our journey toward Heaven. I have never doubted the words that Jesus pronounced at the Last Supper, when He took the bread and wine and said, *"This is my Body,"* and *"This is my Blood"* (Mt 26:26, 28). Each time that the Eucharistic Prayer is said at Mass, and these words of Christ are repeated, I am reminded that in the sacrifice of the Mass the bread and wine become the Body and Blood of Christ, which we receive in Holy Communion. If I believe that Christ died on the Cross to save us from our sins, why should I doubt that the Eucharist is His Body and Blood? I believed this at my First Holy Communion, and I have believed this each and every time that I have received Holy Communion since. And, when I utter my "Amen" before receiving Holy Communion, I am saying that I truly believe that I am receiving the Body and Blood of Christ without any doubt or question!

It has been the constant teaching of the Church that in the sacrifice of the Mass, when the Words of Consecration are repeated by the priest, the bread and wine become the Body and Blood of Christ, yet the appearance of bread and wine remain. However, there have been instances in which even the appearance of the bread and wine has been miraculously changed into the Body and Blood of Christ. About two years after God came to me with The Mission of the Seventy-Two, I witnessed a miracle. I was assisting at the 5 pm Mass, which was celebrated by a visiting priest on a Sunday in Ordinary Time. The priest began the Eucharistic prayer and, in the following words, called down the Holy Spirit upon the gifts, followed by the Words of Consecration:

> Make holy, therefore, these gifts, we pray, by sending down your Spirit upon them like the dewfall, so that they may become for us the Body and Blood of our Lord Jesus Christ. At the time he was betrayed and entered willingly into his Passion, he took bread and giving thanks, broke it, and gave it to his disciples, saying: TAKE THIS, ALL OF YOU, AND EAT OF IT, FOR THIS IS MY BODY, WHICH WILL BE GIVEN UP FOR YOU."

—Eucharistic Prayer II from the Roman Missal

To my utter amazement, and in a moment almost too sacred for words, the celebrant elevated the Host to the assembly, now changed into the Body of Christ, and I saw with my own eyes the face of Christ. The Lord's face was beautifully etched into the grains of the Host. I had the same feeling as when God came to me with The Mission of the Seventy-Two, but this time my experience was visual. I did not tell anyone about what I witnessed because I had to see if this was a one-time occurrence. The following weekend, when I assisted at Mass, I looked intently at the elevated Host and to my astonishment I again saw the face of Christ in the consecrated Host. I have told very few people what I have seen, but I now witness seeing the face of Christ in the consecrated Host at every Mass in which I assist. Every time that I see the face of Christ in the Host, I recall the words of St. Thomas in the Gospel of St. John when he saw Jesus and believed: *"Thomas answered and said to him, 'My Lord and my God!' Jesus said to him, 'Have you come to believe because you have seen me? Blessed are those who have not seen and have believed'"*

(Jn 20:28–29).

For reasons I cannot explain, the image is clearer during some Masses than others. At different times over the last two years, the face of Christ has been so clear that I believe I could have reached out and touched His face with my hands. What I am now telling the world via this writing is the truth of the miracles I have witnessed. I understand that some saints have witnessed or seen Christ in the Eucharist, but I do not consider myself a saint, but a sinner. However, I do consider myself a disciple of Jesus Christ whom the Lord has entrusted with the mission of reaching out to the Good Shepherd's lost sheep.

Even though I continue to receive these miracles at every Mass, this revelation is for the benefit of all the disciples of God's Church because we all receive the same Eucharist, and we all make up the Body of Christ. Christ is in us, and He works through His disciples in a special way within this ministry of The Mission of the Seventy-Two for the purpose of the salvation of lost souls. As St. Paul tells us in the Letter to the Philippians: *"For God is the one who, for his good purpose, works in you both to desire and to work"* (2:13). There can be no purpose for this miracle other than God working in and through His disciples for the salvation of souls.

A year after I saw Christ's face in the consecrated Host, I was again assisting at Mass and was blessed by a second miracle. After singing the Lamb of God, the priest genuflected at the altar and said these words as he held up a section of the broken Host: "Behold the Lamb of God, behold him who takes away the sins of the world. Blessed are those called to the supper of the Lamb" (Roman Missal). At the moment that the piece of the broken Host was elevated over the chalice, I looked intently and clearly saw the same face of Christ in the broken piece of the Host as I had from the whole unbroken Host following the Words of Consecration.

Even though I saw Christ's face in the piece of the Host that was broken off, it is important to remember the teaching of the Church that Christ is present, whole and entire, in the entire Host and in all fragments of the Host. This led me to understand that when Catholics stop attending Mass and separate themselves from the Church it is like the piece of the Host that is broken. When we are baptized, we become members of the Body of Christ, and, when baptized members of the Church are not present, they are still loved by Christ who looks to restore them to His unbroken Body. If some members are missing, then our joy is tempered because the whole body is not present to receive Him in the Eucharist. As baptized members present at the Mass, we need to be the disciples who go forth to make the Church whole again. Then our joy will be complete again because our brothers and sisters will have returned and can share in God's banquet.

Until this day, I continue to see the face of Christ in the Host at every Mass without fail since I first witnessed the face of Christ during that very first Mass. I am blessed to see Christ's face in both the whole and in the fragmented pieces of the Host. This is a further confirmation to me that God is with us and that He wants the Church to be whole again, but that can only happen if His disciples go out into the world to bring inactive Catholics back to the Church. There are many other miraculous things that have happened, but they will not be revealed until I pass from this world into Heaven.

୬ ୬

Conclusion

We Are All Called to Be Shepherds of the Good Shepherd

As part of my research for this book and for The Mission of the Seventy-Two Ministry, I recently reviewed the statistics relevant to weekly Catholic Mass attendance. The most recent CARA statistic indicates the number of Catholics attending Mass on a weekly basis in the United States has dropped from 29% in 2012 to 21.1% in 2018. This represents a significant drop in Mass attendance in only six years within the United States.

We are all called to be shepherds to others, since we are disciples of the one Good Shepherd, Jesus Christ, and, as such, we hear His voice. Bishops, priests, deacons, and religious cannot be the only shepherds. St. Augustine, in a sermon found in the *Liturgy of the Hours,* speaks of pastors, saying:

> All good shepherds are one in the one shepherd.
> . . . All shepherds should therefore be one in the
> good shepherd. All should speak with one voice of
> the one shepherd, so that the sheep may hear and

follow their shepherd; not this or that shepherd but the one shepherd. All should speak with one voice in Christ, not with different voices.

—St. Augustine, *Sermo* 46, 29–30, from the Liturgy of the Hours, Office of Readings, Friday in the 25th Week of Ordinary Time, Second Reading

All active Catholics should speak with one voice proclaiming the Gospel of Jesus Christ and telling the lost sheep that the kingdom of God is at hand. We must not be afraid because the Good Shepherd and the Holy Spirit are with us on our journey. We must not be fearful of alienating our family, friends, neighbors, or fellow Catholics who are away from the Church. The only fear we face is the fear imposed on us by this world, and fear has no place with God.

As shepherds of the Good Shepherd, we must understand what is at stake in the salvation of a lost soul. God is so sorrowful over the loss of one soul to damnation. As St. James tells us: *"My brothers, if anyone among you should stray from the truth and someone bring him back, he should know that whoever brings back a sinner from the error of his way will save his soul from death and will cover a multitude of sins"* (Jas 5:19–20). God sees no failure in our attempt to personally reach out to a lost sheep; the failure occurs when no attempt is made. The attempt is in itself fruitful because the shepherd plants the seed of faith, which may take root in the future according to God's time, not our time.

The most important aspect of our faith lives is the salvation of souls—not just our own soul but the souls of others. Can we even fathom being in Heaven without the ones we love? Can we love God with our entire being if our neighbor does not recognize the love of God? St. Vincent de Paul, a companion of St. Francis de Sales, who brought back many fallen-away Catholics, said the following:

> Our vocation is to go, not just to one parish, not just to one diocese, but all over the world; and to do what? To set people's hearts on fire, to do what the Son of God did. He came to set the world on fire in order to inflame it with His love. What do we have to desire but that it may burn and consume everything. . . . It's true then, that I'm sent not only to love God but to make Him loved. It's not enough for me to love God, if my neighbor doesn't love Him.
>
> —Vincent de Paul, May 30, 1659 (SV XII, 215)

The Mission of the Seventy-Two is so important that every parish, not only in every diocese, and not only in the United States, but in the entire world, should have some form of this ministry. I'm not saying that this ministry of The Mission of the Seventy-Two has all of the answers because it doesn't. But I know that there are many shepherds and disciples in the world who have the hearts, the souls, and the minds to draw strength from the Good Shepherd to go out into the world and bring back the lost sheep of the Church. Active disciples of the Church, shepherds of the Good Shepherd, must make it their priority to bring back the inactive members so the number of lost sheep doesn't increase from where it stands right now, and it will if nothing is done. The enemy is winning souls every day, and the faithful cannot let this happen because the salvation of souls is at stake. The Church needs to win battles one soul at a time because God will eventually win the war.

We must never give up on inviting the lost sheep to the Church. We must keep fighting the good fight in the battle for the salvation of souls. The reason for never giving up is that God never gives up on us; we must remain steadfast in our mission to invite inactive Catholics to the Church—the salvation of their souls is at stake.

St. Asterius of Amasea said, in part, the following in his homily entitled "Be shepherds like the Lord": "Let us look more closely at the hidden meaning of this parable. The sheep is more than a sheep, the shepherd more than a shepherd. They are examples enshrining holy truths. They teach us that we should not look on men as lost or beyond hope; we should not abandon them when they are in danger or be slow to come to their help. When they turn away from the right path and wander, we must lead them back, and rejoice at their return, welcoming them back into the company of those who lead good and holy lives" (Liturgy of the Hours, Thursday of the First Week of Lent: Hom. 13: PG 40, 355–358, 362).

At the end of Mass we have the final blessing and dismissal: "Go in peace; glorifying the Lord by your life." Having taken to heart God's Word and having been nourished with Christ's

Body, Blood, Soul, and Divinity in the Eucharist, we must now take Him out into the world to make a difference in the lives of the lost sheep, and there are definitely more lost sheep than shepherds. As Jesus tells us in the Gospel of St. Luke:

"The harvest is abundant but the laborers are few; so ask the master of the harvest to send out laborers for his harvest" (10:2).

The Good Shepherd has a plan for you, His shepherds, to commission you to bring back His many wandering sheep.

The Shepherd's Commission

There is only one Good Shepherd, Jesus Christ, the keeper of the gate,

But as His Disciple let me emulate the Good Shepherd in this world.

My desire is to walk in His footsteps as I draw closer to Him.

Let me not be afraid to reach out to His lost sheep, who have wandered away from His flock.

Give me courage, wisdom and strength against the evil one who has led His sheep to only what this world has to offer.

Let me make the necessary sacrifice in charity filled with compassion and love to reach out to the lost ones, who have squandered His blessings and misused His graces.

75

Let the lost sheep look into the merciful gaze of the Good Shepherd's disciple and see the forgiveness He has awaiting them on their return.

Give me a shepherd's heart that will ache until His lost sheep have been found.

The Good Shepherd
by Jean Baptiste de Champaigne
(1631–1681)

Give me the soul that yearns to know my mission and that it will not be complete until all of the lost are returned to the road of salvation.

Let my heart rejoice, my soul be enveloped in thanksgiving and give all glory and praise to the Good Shepherd when His lost sheep come home to His loving embrace. Amen.

Returning a soul to the Church is a miracle because the person continues on his or her journey to salvation and to the sacraments of the Church. Such a miracle is met with much rejoicing both in Heaven and on earth. We read in the Gospel of St. Luke: *"And when he does find it, he sets it on his shoulders with great joy and, upon arrival home, he calls together his friends and neighbors and says to them, 'Rejoice with me because I have found my lost sheep'"* (Lk 15:5–6).

Now that you have finished this book, I would like to ask you three questions, similar to those that I posed to you in the Introduction:

- What is the Good Shepherd asking or calling you to do in bringing back His lost sheep to His Church?
- As a shepherd of the Good Shepherd, after hearing His voice, would you venture out into the world to look for His lost sheep?
- Would you allow the Good Shepherd to embrace your heart and soul to make it a priority in your life to bring back the lost sheep to His Church?

My prayer for you is that you are not afraid to reach out to the lost souls of the Church. Just as the Father sent Jesus, Jesus is sending you.

May God bless and keep you, giving you the heart and soul of the Good Shepherd.

Acknowledgement

I give all praise and glory to God for the The Mission of the Seventy-Two ministry. This ministry is His, not mine. I am His servant, His disciple, a shepherd of the Good Shepherd just wanting to save souls and bring them back to the Church. I know He is with me and because of this, I am not afraid. I will continue in this mission until I join Him in Heaven. I will not give up on any inactive Catholic because God does not give up on us. Just like the seventy-two disciples that were hand-picked by Jesus, my hope is that God will bring disciples from around the world in the fight for the salvation of souls. I thank God for letting me be a part of His mission.

CPSIA information can be obtained
at www.ICGtesting.com
Printed in the USA
JSHW011949020723
44052JS00003B/16